WORK FROM HOME WHILE YOU ROAM

The Ultimate Work From Home Guide

Rebecca T. Hall

Table Of Contents

CHAPTER FIVE
Conclusion

INTRODUCTION

In the early 1900s, it was considered a luxury to work from home. Technology has advanced significantly over the past century, a blessing for us. Most businesses now accept remote applicants for their jobs and allow them to work remotely as part of the hiring process. Even if remote work is not your current goal, it's worth learning how to work remotely and make it enjoyable.

CHAPTER ONE

WHAT DOES IT MEAN TO WORK FROM HOME?

Keeping in touch with your current work in a globalized world can be challenging. It's not an option to work from home; it is becoming preferred when traditional office space is physically prohibitive, too expensive, or just plain impossible. It's becoming more common for people to consider working remotely part of their career.

There are many advantages to working from home beyond the convenience factor. Working from home is an option in today's global economy. For the following reasons:

A Healthy Work-life Balance

You can have a superior balance between fun and serious activities by working from home. This allows you to reduce commute time, spend more time with your family, and avoid the distractions of office politics. It is possible to work around the school or child's schedules. You are also able to adapt your work hours to suit them. This option is popular among professionals as it saves them the hassle of job hunting in an environment with high unemployment and increasing job scarcity.

A Healthier Environment

You have complete control over the environment where you work when you work remotely. You can choose the privacy, quiet, or lifestyle that suits your needs. The workspace you choose will reflect your style and personality. However, it is possible to avoid compromising that the workplace is shared with other office-mates. This can be a competitive advantage that helps keep office politics away.

More freedom and flexibility

Working from home gives you more flexibility and freedom than in traditional office settings because you can move around in your workspace according to what is most convenient for the task at hand. You can also set your hours and have complete control over your earning potential.

Increased Productivity

It's easier to focus your attention and keep your head clear when working remotely. Because distractions aren't always at your doorstep, you will be more productive. You will be more productive if you work from home.

Communication has increased

You can communicate with clients from your home 24/7. This eliminates time zones and time difference barriers. This is a great competitive advantage. You can communicate with clients and colleagues at any time.

THE BEST WAY TO GET STARTED WITH WORKING FROM HOME

First, ensure reliable internet access if you plan to work from home. While fast broadband is the best option, if your connection slows down during peak hours, it can affect your ability to work. It doesn't matter what you have - all that is required is an internet connection capable of at least 10Mbps (megabits per sec).

It's also a good idea if your window looks out onto the greenery or towards the sky. This will allow you to feel less cramped and give you the chance to get some natural light throughout the day.

If you want to work from home and are not sure where to start, look for a job that meets the following criteria:

1. **It is remote.** It should be possible to do it from home at a time that works for you.

2. **It should be a match for your skills and experience.** You might be able to find a job as an

assistant virtual if you have a background in business administration and you are currently working as a secretary.

3. You should enjoy it or be passionate about it. Even if your current job is not what you love, you can still see the potential for a new career. Another option is to look in an entirely different industry than the one you are familiar with but have always wanted to be involved in.

4. You must be willing to work for it, either in commission or salary. You might consider home-based jobs that pay generously and don't require much work if you need to make more than the average salary to live comfortably.

5. This role must be one you can handle yourself and allow for ample time.

6. You should be able to do it from your home. However, if you need to travel, it should still pay well.

CHAPTER TWO

GENUINE REMOTE WORK OPPORTUNITIES

HOW TO EARN MONEY WORKING FROM HOME

There are numerous methods to make money while working from home, regardless of whether you're searching for a full-time job or a side hustle to supplement your income. Making money from home has numerous advantages, including the freedom to choose your hours and the ability to maintain a healthy work-life balance.

Here are several legal ways to work from home and make additional money, get a second job, start a full-time solo profession, or start your own small business.

Financial empowerment apps might help you find new sources of income: You need **Steady**—a financial empowerment software that links you with chances to grow and diversify your income—whether you currently have an at-home side business (or full-fledged business) or are still looking into methods to earn more on your own time. The program claims that Steady Members make an additional $5,000 a year, and Steady has already given out more than $10 million in financial rewards. It also assisted Members in obtaining emergency cash assistance totaling at least $4 million.

Flexible and individualized earning opportunities are offered by Steady. You'll start receiving personalized income recommendations and insights from the growing Steady Member community after providing some basic information about yourself and finishing your profile. Furthermore, Steady collaborates with trustworthy outside organizations who provide genuine cash rewards, or "Income Boosters," when you make wiser financial decisions. Additionally, with comprehensive data collected from the local community, you can keep track of what other Steady members are making in your region as well as what local employers are paying.

With the Steady app, users reportedly make, on average, almost $5,000 more annually. That's a lot of cash. Additionally, Steady has provided more than $10 million in monetary incentives while also arranging for another $4 million in urgent cash assistance (and counting).

Blogging: Market Your Analysis:

Blogs aren't just places where bored folks vent about anything and everything. Aspiring bloggers looking to earn money online may also find them to be a reliable source of revenue. A concept is the first step in your blogging journey. If your idea isn't fully original, it must at least be more appealing and crisp than those of your rivals. This is a crucial early decision for your blog.

You should be completely knowledgeable on the topic of your blog, ideally gained from personal experience or formal education, and be able to write about it with ease. With practice, you'll be able to write more quickly and with higher quality. Then the details: picking and purchasing a Web domain, hosting and developing your site, and organizing content. Even though there is a lot of work to be done before publishing your first post, resist the urge to skimp. Hopefully, you're setting the stage for a sustained effort. There are several ways to monetize your blog once you've built a high-quality site and a loyal audience.

Selling Your Expertise Through Online Tutoring:

By sharing your subject-matter expertise online, you can make money more intimately through virtual tutoring. Tutoring sessions are frequently one-on-one encounters, in contrast to online courses, which are accessible to dozens or even hundreds of paying consumers at once. The number of students you can have depends on your schedule.

Similar to online teaching, focus on topics you are an expert in to increase your chances of being a successful online teacher. Use a respected location with plenty of visibility, thoughtfully plan your sessions, charge a fair price for your offerings, adhere to best practices for scheduling, and aggressively sell yourself. The best locations to look for online tutoring employment are tutoring-specific platforms like **Education First** and **Chegg**. Both pay pre-determined hourly or session fees based on the tutors' chosen disciplines; for example, computer science tutors typically make more money than English tutors. **Chegg** claims that successful tutors can make up to $1,000 per month. They start at $20 per hour.

Selling Your Words as a Freelancer:

Numerous Americans, ranging from retirees to high school and college students, make additional money writing for clients. If you have a way with words, writing blog posts and web copy is a simple and enjoyable method to supplement your full-time income.

Although challenging, getting started as a freelance writer is possible. With general-purpose freelancing platforms like **Upwork** and writing-only portals like **Textbroker**, there are numerous freelance writing positions available at the lowest end of the wage scale. While the writing chances on these platforms are frequently boring (plenty of product descriptions, ad content, and press releases) and don't pay well at all, it will help you learn what editors want from freelance writers and hone your writing skills in the process.

Experiment outside of your comfort zone as you develop experience (and confidence) as a freelance writer. Don't be hesitant to raise your charges for freelance writing, create contracts to safeguard yourself from dishonest clients, and send out queries to publications where you'd be glad to see your byline. No matter how great you are, rejection is a part of the freelance writing game. However, if you are persistent, you'll hear "yes" more frequently than you anticipate.

Selling Your Grammar Skills: Freelance Editing and Proofreading:

Freelance editing and proofreading are a natural result of freelance writing. While not all writers are naturally gifted editors or proofreaders, the two abilities frequently go hand in hand.

Freelance Editing: You'll probably have a sense of the abilities and responsibilities necessary for the position after working with a few different editors. Finding suitable editing jobs is then all that remains.

Start modestly as a new editor. Look for project-based or part-time copy editing positions. Utilize current agreements for freelance writing if at all possible.

When your current clientele is no longer sufficient, consider applying to positions on online job sites like **Upwork** and media-specific platforms like **Mediabistro**. Online editing jobs typically come in the following forms:

• **Copy Editor.** Copy editors frequently operate as the primary point of contact for contributing writers and make sure written material is polished before their superiors hit "publish." Copy editing is sometimes a stepping stone to more lucrative editing or production possibilities, although it isn't particularly well compensated.

• **Assistant Editor.** Copy editors, photo editors, writers, and other support personnel who work on producing digital publications are under the supervision of assistant editors. Larger blogs and online-print hybrids typically employ at least one assistant editor. These jobs can be full- or part-time. They usually fall in between managing editing projects and copy editing.

• **Managing Editor.** Lower-level editors who work on editorial teams are under the supervision and management of managing editors. Even though these jobs are more difficult to get and take up more of your time, temporary positions look fantastic on resumes. Start with smaller blogs and specialized magazines with minimal budgets and few content requirements if you don't have much formal editing expertise. Some newspapers don't have enough work for a full-time editor, making it possible to tie together a few part-time editing jobs or try out one position to see how it suits you.

• **Web/Photo Editor.** Visuals that appear on websites and other digital media, such as white papers and business reports, are produced or edited by photo and web editors. Working in this field is an excellent chance to develop your visual talents and gain experience with layout and editing software like WordPress and Photoshop. These jobs frequently call for beginner to advanced coding abilities, making them ideal for independent contractors looking to diversify their skill set beyond writing.

• **Editor of Manuscripts.** In search of a long - term commitment? Manuscript editors, professionals who assist authors in organizing and honing book-length works before publication, are in high demand as a result of the self-publishing boom. Manuscript editing can be financially rewarding, but it may take some time to establish your reputation to the point where you are hiring experienced authors. There are numerous entry-level positions available with respected freelance platforms and specialized publishing companies.

Freelance Proofreading:

Although they share many of the same talents and abilities as independent writers and editors, their professional trajectories are different.

Even with prior writing or editing experience, enrolling in a proofreading course will help someone new to the freelance proofreading game get off to the best start possible and build credibility with potential clients. A good example is **Proofread Anywhere**. There is no commitment if you decide the gig isn't for you with free introductory modules.

The majority of proofreading jobs fall into one of two broad categories: general proofreading or technical proofreading, despite the remarkable diversity of the sector. The former includes non-technical, broadly categorized media such as blogs and books. The latter includes proofreading for transcripts and other technical materials; court reporters, for instance, are skilled proofreaders. Which one you pick will rely on your natural talents as a proofreader and what you hope to gain from the position. Technical proofreading is more competitive but often pays higher than ordinary proofreading; it is also tougher to get started.

Digital books and audiobooks Achieve New Heights in Your Writing (or Acting) Career

After a while, even the most dedicated freelance writers become bored and dejected. Consider taking on lengthy projects that challenge your creativity and have significant passive revenue possibilities if you're sick of creating Web material or blog posts for clients or you just want to broaden your horizons.

Although reading and hearing your name in print is a commendable accomplishment in and of itself, selling audiobooks is unlikely to make you wealthy. The majority of the time, your royalty-sharing agreement will only cost a few dollars per download.

How well you market your audiobook and how visible it is on outlets like Audible and iTunes will have a big impact. A successful audiobook could, with some luck, provide a five-figure income stream each year. Capturing Your Work

You can use an entirely new source of income if you already have a book written by converting it into an audiobook. The voice on the recording doesn't have to be yours. It's preferable to hire a trained voice actor unless you have prior voice acting or radio experience.

Reputable platforms like **ACX** frequently feature affordable production expenses and creative royalty-sharing structures that enhance the cash possibilities for rights-holders (authors). To get a list of available platforms, visit Publishers Weekly.

Capturing the work of others

You can use **ACX** and other resources to obtain audiobook recording jobs if you have experience as a voice actor or narrator or believe you have what it takes to break into the industry. Each role requires an audition, but once you get the job, you'll get paid twice: once at an agreed-upon hourly rate for the actual work, and once through a shared royalty deal with the rights-holder and other people engaged in the production.

If you're an actor in the union (SAG-AFTRA), you must charge a minimum rate (varying, but over

$200) every completed hour (roughly two studio hours). That works up to a minimum wage of $2,000 before royalties for a 10-hour audiobook.

Paid social media posts: Earn Money by Sharing, Pinning, and Tweeting

Forging a following on social media does not require having millions of users. You only need to adhere to the fundamental social media etiquette guidelines and locate a trustworthy platform that pays you to distribute sponsored material from its users or to advertise affiliate goods.

Try one of these approaches if you're serious about creating genuine, long-term money on social media:

Partner Program for YouTube

YouTube channel owners can now monetize specific kinds of videos thanks to the YouTube Partner program.

It takes time and effort to discover corporations ready to pay for direct or indirect promotion, and you need to build up a significant following before you can find paying ads. Furthermore, your videos need to adhere to YouTube's monetization requirements, which forbid explicit or plagiarized material.

Your channel's subscriber count and, to a lesser extent, the demographics of your audience, determine your earning potential.

Affiliate marketing

Affiliate marketing can make money from your social media platforms in addition to your blog or website. Numerous affiliate marketers combine the two.

The best place to begin is **ClickBank**. Pay is strongly correlated with the number of followers and the demographics of your audience.

Sell Your Organizational Skills as Virtual Assistant Services

The resources or office space needed to hire an on-site assistant are frequently not available to busy professionals and small business owners. Many people opt to engage virtual assistants (VAs) on a part-time or contract basis to reap the advantages of having a dependable assistant without incurring the costs and administrative hassles of a full-time employee.

The normal responsibilities of a virtual assistant are as follows:

• Screening calls, taking and replying to messages, and providing the customer with crucial information.

• Managing, planning, and creating content for social media, email marketing, and websites.

• Basic administrative and clerical activities.

• Compiling and running reports.

• Managing e-commerce operations, including fulfillment.

The following tools are required or advised:

• A convenient workstation and workspace.

• A standardized and expandable electronic organization system.

• A quick Internet connection.

• A secure email program.

• Malware protection.

• A virtual private network (VPN) from **NordVPN**, especially if anonymity is a concern or you're working with clients outside of your home country.

• Permissions and passwords for the primary accounts to which you have access.

• A dependable phone setup (either a landline or a cloud-based business phone system), preferably with a headset.

• A secure method of invoicing and receiving payment, like **FreshBooks** or PayPal.

Virtual assistants can devote as little as a few hours per customer every week, either all at once or evenly spaced out. Since there is enough work, it is simple to combine several gigs into a full- or nearly full-time position. Start looking for virtual assistant jobs on general-purpose freelance sites like Upwork, **Fiverr**, and **Freelancer**, but think about building your website.

Selling Your Viewing Time While Watching TV and Online Videos

If you enjoy watching TV shows, web videos, or both, you can make money from your hobby.

Compared to other chances, some pay more generously and consistently. According to reports, Netflix pays "taggers," who watch and categorize Netflix shows, at least $10 per hour. Although these possibilities are dwindling and getting harder to find, occasionally individual shows or production companies will post for similar positions. When jobs do become available, competition is fierce.

Other opportunities are more accessible but far less rewarding. Many market research firms offer verticals for watching videos where participants may accumulate points for each view. Two trustworthy choices that let users swap points for gift cards and occasionally cash are **Swagbucks** and **InboxDollars**.

In most situations, hourly wages come out to be less than minimum wage, but they're still not bad for a few free minutes here and there.

Invest in Your Future with Tech Work

Contrary to popular assumption, not all well-paying non-college positions are hazardous or taxing. Some can be completed from the convenience of your home office with nothing more than a high-end laptop and a fast Internet connection.

Of course, you also need the proper abilities. With a Bootcamp from Springboard, a top provider of tech certification courses, you may increase your earning potential in industries like UI/UX and data analytics, where full-time incomes for entry-level jobs easily reach $50,000 per year.

Although Springboard isn't free, it does have a backup plan: it will reimburse your course fees if you can't find a job after looking for one actively for six months after graduation. For an investment that may genuinely change the direction of your career, that's not a bad value.

Although Codecademy's money-back guarantee is less substantial than Springboard's, it has a much larger course catalog. Take the quiz to find out how your current talents fit into the vast (and frequently perplexing) world of programming if you're not sure where to begin.

Accommodations: Let a Room in Your House

Are you getting the most money out of your house? The answer is probably no if your mother-in-law's suite, duplex unit, or spare bedroom is vacant.

You can generate cash from the spare space in your home without having to find a long-term tenant. You can rent out your house to business and leisure tourists on a nightly or weekly basis using apps like Airbnb, Vrbo, and HomeAway.

You may make anywhere from $40 or $50 to $500 or more per night, depending on local market rents, the size, amenities, and privacy of your apartment.

Short-term rental platforms handle most of the thorny logistical factors that prohibit typical homeowners from becoming landlords, including payment processing and security deposits.

Additionally, these platforms are becoming more safety-conscious as a result of a spate of widely publicized accidents in their early years, increasing the possibility that you will be able to identify every person who crashes at your location.

Naturally, not all homes are prepared for renting. Consider the following factors before listing your property on websites like Airbnb and Vrbo:

Stranger Risk

What's most important is that you and your family members decide whether you feel comfortable having guests around. This is less of a problem if you have a separate entry for your second unit, but it still merits careful thought.

Municipal Rules

Even if local governments are becoming more open to short-term rentals, there are still some opponents. Surprisingly, tourism towns occasionally voice their opposition the loudest. Follow local laws as they change. Make sure you pay all necessary municipal and state hospitality taxes if your city does permit short-term rentals.

Pets

Short-term rental agreements are complicated by dogs and cats. Giving someone complete access to your home is difficult when you're concerned that they might unintentionally let Fido or Fluffy out when they return in the middle of the night.

To avoid a poison review on your otherwise spotless internet listing from an allergic tenant, you need at the very least declare that you have dogs.

Damage and Cleaning

You can set up cleaning fees on online rental platforms so that you won't be financially responsible for the whole expense of a post-tenant professional cleaning. Most insurance policies also cover damage caused by renters as long as you properly document and report it.

But monetary compensation only goes so far. You still have to cope with the unavoidable time and energy commitment required to repair the harm or clear up the resulting mess.

Direct Hosting

You don't have to act as the guests' tour guide, but you do need to be approachable and ready to assist if a situation occurs.

Short-term rental hosting might not be your greatest option for at-home income if you're not prepared to put down what you're doing or at the very least pick up the phone to assist a tenant in need.

Renting a car: Use your vehicle

Don't have a spare room or extra apartment you could rent out each night? Without getting behind the wheel or even leaving your home, you can rent out your vehicle to tourists and those who don't own cars.

There are many apps available for renting a car. Read the fine print carefully before selecting one, and confirm that it has sufficient liability insurance to safeguard you in the event of a catastrophic collision resulting in injuries and property damage.

Getaround has a solid reputation and a respectable amount of experience. According to the company's website, automobile owners in highly populated areas like San Francisco can make up to $10,000 annually. Another trustworthy option is **Turo**, which touts possible revenues per car of up to $10,000 a year. That is a very strong passive revenue source.

Technical Assistance: Sell Your Problem-Solving Techniques

Do you enjoy interacting with others? Do you possess superior technical expertise, a willingness to learn, or both?

If that's the case, you might be a good technical support agent. While many technical support and customer service representatives still work in centralized contact centers, at-home employees have various opportunities.

At-Home Counselors

Apple, whose At Home Advisor program employs thousands of individuals at competitive, experience-based rates, is one of the largest and best-known at-home tech support businesses.

Since At Home Advisors are part- or full-time employees rather than independent contractors, there is a level of security there that is frequently lacking from work-at-home opportunities. Every At Home Advisor receives a complimentary iMac as part of the perks package, which also includes Apple shares.

The drawback is that the hiring process is very competitive, so you'll probably need to show that you have experience or leave a strong impression on the hiring manager.

If hired, you will have to finish a paid, five to seven-week training program. You'll also need to spend money on a legitimate home office, which Apple defines as "a quiet, distraction-free room with a door that can close to keep out ambient noise... a desk, an ergonomic chair, and your high-speed Internet connection from a reliable provider that meets the minimum requirements of 5 megabits per second download and 1 megabit per second upload."

Sell solutions to people's queries on question marketplaces

Many queries can be found online. You might get paid if you can answer them in an informed and objective manner.

Answers to questions submitted by community members are paid for via online question marketplaces. If you are an expert in a given field or subject, you could generate a solid side income by simply imparting your knowledge.

JustAnswer is one of the most dependable and successful online question marketplaces. Health, home renovation, automobiles, law, business, technology, pets, and homework are some of the verticals covered by **JustAnswer**. You require pertinent legal or accounting degrees to work in the majority of sectors.

Although compensation varies by vertical, it seems to be quite generous. Depending on your area of expertise, you may make between $2,000 and $7,000 per month, according to **JustAnswer**.

You might not initially find as much work as you anticipate because your workload is dependent on the quality of your responses and the number of queries customers are asking. Nevertheless, **JustAnswer** lends itself well to multitasking, making it the ideal work-from-home option.

Wonder is one more choice that doesn't call for official credentials. **Wonder** is coy about how much it pays, but customer pricing for finished queries starts at around $40, so contributors probably receive at least half of that. Your earning potential is, however, constrained by Wonder's seeming lower question volume compared to **JustAnswer**.

Webinars and Classes: Promote Education

For regular people who wish to offer their thoughts and affect businesses' decision-making processes, online surveys and focus groups are fantastic. What about individuals with genuine subject matter expertise, or at the very least, above-average talents in a discipline that is in demand?

You may teach students and make money doing it without getting hired as an adjunct professor at your community college. You can bypass the middleman and deliver lessons directly to lifelong learners without ever leaving your home thanks to the wonders of the Internet.

To launch and run a successful at-home teaching business, remember the following:

Credibility

When you have some credibility, selling your knowledge will go more smoothly. Formal credentials are almost always required in numerous fields. To learn from a CPA, students enroll in a course on online tax preparation. A lawyer or serial entrepreneur is the person entrepreneurs seek out when they want the inside scoop on small-business law.

Venue

Pick trustworthy, well-known locations for your classes while you're just starting. You shouldn't anticipate that students will visit your personal or professional website before you have established a solid reputation.

For aspiring at-home instructors wishing to make a living from their business, **Udemy** is a fantastic alternative. Another good alternative is **YouTube**, although you can't charge people to watch your films there. They'll need to be indirectly monetized.

Issue and Organization

A well-liked vertical is not sufficient. Each lesson should have an interesting subject and a clear outline. Everyone wants to learn how to write, but you can't cover all the common programming languages in one hour.

Create your course offerings on popular, specialist themes that are of interest to students. Use practical examples, interactive activities, and eye-catching visuals (whiteboards are effective) whenever possible.

Costs and Promotions

You should determine the value of your teaching abilities and set a fair price for them, just like you would with any other career.

You may locate someone who bills less for comparable labor because at-home teaching is, unfortunately, a competitive industry. Multicourse discounts, package offers, and gifts or information for early enrollees are all ways to get around this.

Promotion

You don't need to spend money on digital advertisements to advertise your lessons, but it will be worthwhile to solicit support through social media, email (sending out targeted blasts to your professional and personal networks), and email.

Reputable online learning communities like **Udemy** will increase your visibility as you attract more students, taking some of the burdens off your promotional efforts. You must choose to join its enormous course marketing network, though.

Many of these work-from-home alternatives entail either passive income or side businesses that aren't likely to become full-time activities. However, some of them, like freelance writing and editing, are easily scalable.

Nothing is stopping you from converting your at-home side business into a full-time career if you're prepared to hit the pavement in search of paid clients and are competent with productivity advice for remote workers.

WORK FROM HOME SCAMS – **HOW TO AVOID THESE PHONY JOB OPPORTUNITIES**

HOW TO AVOID WORK-FROM-HOME SCAMS

It can be very tempting to raise income through active and passive income streams, particularly in difficult economic circumstances and for individuals who aren't currently working full-time. Scam artists with a sense of initiative take advantage of our innate desire to increase the financial value of our job. If they are successful, we are left in worse conditions than before, both materially and psychologically.

Many work-at-home scams adopt recognizable, simple-to-recognize shapes, while individual frauds frequently appear and vanish before the authorities can catch them. The following are examples of typical work-from-home scams:

• "Middleman" possibilities, such as sending parcels or cashing checks for a third party

• Home assembly and manufacturing

• Pyramid techniques

• Insufficiently defined "business opportunities"

- Activities in the gray area, such as mystery shopping and medical billing, which occasionally are legitimate but frequently aren't

Medico-Legal Billing

Some medical billing specialists who work from home have solid employment, but the job market is cutthroat, and there are many more frauds than real openings. Take caution no matter how alluring the opportunity may seem.

Usually, victims of fraudulent medical billing opportunities are required to pay upfront for expensive software, training materials, or lead lists that they are told are necessary. However, the material's total worth is greatly exaggerated.

Other common issues include the software itself not functioning as promised and the lead lists consisting of hospitals and clinics rather than specifically targeted lists of medical professionals who have expressed interest in billing services.

Creating a Personal Online Business

This con sounds like a dream come true: a plug-and-play business you can manage and scale without ever leaving the house, generating thousands of dollars per month in no time at all.

There is only one catch: Before getting started, you must pay for professional "coaching" and other nebulous services that are allegedly necessary for your success. When all is said and done, these services can run into the thousands.

Even if they are delivered, they are of no use at all because the worst of these con artists simply pocket their victims' money without giving them anything in return. These "services" frequently just offer information that you may acquire on the internet by conducting an independent investigation.

One distinguishing trait of Internet business fraud is high-pressure sales. Scammers relentlessly encourage people who indicate interest in their offers to act quickly before it's too late by claiming that they are only accessible for a short time.

Cashing Checks & Wiring

Cashing check scams are also straightforward but can have disastrous results for victims.

Fraud involving international payment processing is one of the most prevalent variations. The victim of this scam is asked to open a bank account, cash fraudulent checks for clients from abroad, and wire the majority of the money (minus a processing fee for the victim) to a third party. The victim is left holding the bag legally and financially when the bank realizes the check is phony.

Entry of data

Another occasionally acceptable work-from-home job that is frequently fraudulent is data input (or misleading, at minimum).

When it comes to expensive software that doesn't work and training materials that don't offer anything new, fraudulent medical billing chances and illegal data input possibilities frequently resemble one another.

Real data entry jobs often feature corporate-provided training rather than self-directed instruction and don't demand prior payment because the corporation gives the software for free.

Multilevel marketing schemes

Multilevel marketing (MLM) schemes can be profitable, just as mystery shopping and medical billing. However, they frequently mislead and take advantage of people, which severely disadvantages subsequent comers (those on the lowest tiers of the system).

It can be difficult to distinguish between genuine MLMs and explicit pyramid scams (even ones that may be exploitative). Avoid any MLM that prioritizes bringing on new "subs" – those higher up the ladder — over selling genuine goods.

Packaging Envelopes

One of the oldest and most straightforward work-from-home frauds is envelope stuffing.

The traditional envelope-stuffing scam requests a minimal fee from victims to teach them how to stuff and send envelopes for money from the comfort of their own homes. By distributing advertisements for the same envelope-stuffing fraud to others, they enlist in a crude pyramid scheme in exchange.

The majority of the time, victims of envelope stuffing only get paid when a recipient accepts the offer, which is uncommon. Even with postage and sending expenses, any earnings are unlikely to cover the initial launch price.

The "employer" who presents the opportunity does not profit, but that is fine. They've already kept the initial charge, and they keep running ads on free websites like Craigslist and spam email.

By using victims to market their goods or services, a common variation of this scam cheats the employer. In such circumstances, the envelope's contents are merely advertisements for whatever the employer is marketing.

Sending packages

This con looks straightforward enough. The only requirement is for the participant to reply to the offer with their address, wait for a box from Amazon or another online merchant to arrive, and then the shipment is delivered to a third address.

It is easy to fall for the hoax. Participants can also risk legal repercussions as a result. Since identity thieves frequently utilize package forwarding victims as fronts to hide their genuine names and whereabouts, this is the case.

The packages are bought by the con artist using stolen credit card or bank account information, who then sends them to the addresses of unwary victims to elude law authorities.

A public address, like a UPS Store, is usually used by scammers to pick up their parcels, which puts the victims in legal trouble.

Sending Emails

This fraud is an updated version of the traditional stuffing of envelopes scam.

The initial pitch, which is frequently sent by email, promotes the possibility of making quick cash through an opportunity involving email marketing. The victim is required to pay up in advance for training materials or software that the con artist claims are necessary for getting the task done.

In certain circumstances, the con artist simply takes the money from the victims and leaves. In some cases, they only send an enlarged version of the initial pitch with the request that you forward it to everyone in your address book.

It might be worse than useless if there is any software involved. Sometimes the dangerous malware or adware used in these scams can affect your computer's functionality or aid in identity theft.

Assembly and Manufacturing Done at Home

For those who prefer using their hands, so-called craft scams look like an alluring opportunity.

They aren't. They are a waste of time and money.

Craft con artists demand hundreds of dollars (and often even more) from their victims in exchange for specialized assembly tools, such as the best sewing machines or printing apparatuses, and the "high-quality" materials required to make the claimed crafts. They promise a hefty payment in return for each completed piece.

Some con artists that target crafters simply take their victims' money and run, never bothering to supply fake tools and supplies. Others do follow through on their original promises, but the price of whatever they give is likely to be far less than the victim's first payment.

They continue to reject finished products because they don't fulfill strict quality requirements, squandering the victim's valuable time for hours before the victim eventually learns his lesson.

You Are Required to Make an Initial Investment or Supply Payment Information

Opportunities to work from home that demand payment upfront for anything — tools, supplies, software, training materials, or anything else — are virtually always fraudulent.

Legitimate MLMs are a limited exception, but only if the sponsor of the opportunity can explain in great detail how the business makes money. If not, work-from-home positions that need upfront payments are ideally used as channels by scammers to market highly inflated goods or information. In the worst-case scenario, they serve as fronts for thieves attempting to steal credit card details.

The Offer Makes Outlandish Claims About the Potential for Passive Income

Be wary of any offer that is long on claims of enormous passive income with little effort and short on details of how to get there.

Dreamy stock photographs of "workers" lounging on a Tahitian beach or squeezing Swiss powder don't tell you anything about the actual job, which is a lot less beautiful in reality, assuming it even exists.

Several chances that are virtually always fake are included in this widespread work-from-home scam, like check forwarding and in-home assembly.

It also contains possibilities that fall between being genuinely authentic and being completely false. Some billing and mystery-shopping gigs are lucrative. Higher-level multilevel marketing participants frequently do fairly well for themselves.

Other employment options, such as conducting online surveys through Survey Junkie and taking part in digital focus groups or product testing panels, offer home-based employees additional earning potential.

It's unfair to label these possibilities as scams when many of them are authentic. However, anyone considering them needs to be aware that they won't make them wealthy.

In actuality, that is sound advice for anyone looking for any way to get extra money. It doesn't make it worthwhile to spend your time just because you can use it to enhance your income.

CHAPTER THREE

QUICKSTART JOBS GUIDE

IS A REMOTE JOB THE RIGHT FIT FOR YOU?

It's crucial to decide whether working remotely is a good fit for you before beginning. While working from home may seem like a dream come true, it demands a lot of self-discipline and isn't for everyone. Before choosing a profession that allows you to work from home, think about the following questions:

1. **How significant is social interaction in my line of work?** Although many remote professions offer communication tools like Slack and Zoom, depending on your job type and the time of day, you might not contact anyone. This may seem like a benefit to some, but many people find it difficult to spend extended periods with few people.

2. How is life at home? Many people find it isolating to work from home, especially if they live alone. Think about your daily routine at home and try to visualize spending an additional eight hours there. If you don't go out often, would staying in more make you feel lonely? Or will work from home provide you the alone time you need if you're swamped with household duties (such as taking the kids to after-school activities, chores, hanging out with friends, etc.)?

3. How would my job be structured? Working from home can seem extremely different depending on the position you're looking for. A freelance writer, for instance, could find it simpler to focus at home, away from interruptions and coworkers. A therapist may find it more difficult to recognize facial clues or warning signs during sessions. Every profession has a method for increasing production from home, but bear in mind that to be effective, you might need to alter the way you carry out your duties.

A FEW GUIDELINES

Once you've decided to work from home, you'll need to make some adjustments to your home to get ready for your new position. This advice will assist you in better distinguishing between your personal and professional lives if you've never worked from home full-time.

1. Look for a designated workstation.

Whether you work full- or part-time, it is essential to designate a specific workstation within your house to carry out your obligations. Keeping your "working life" apart from your personal life can be accomplished by designating a regular workspace. If you live with family members or roommates, this may be especially crucial. They won't bother you all day if you have a location where they can see you are working.

It's not necessary to have a spare room to set up a workspace. All you need to do is carve aside a little workspace in your home, like a desk or table. To make your desk area as private as possible, you can move furniture around to make it more of a distinct location or spend money on a divider.

2. Maintain regular business hours.

If you've never done remote work, you might believe that this job will allow you to work fewer hours. Unfortunately, not all remote employees can say this. It may be difficult to ever feel like you are "off the clock" if there are no set office hours or a spot to punch in and out. It's relatively simple to work more hours than necessary, which might result in a poor work-life balance.

Maintaining regular office hours is one strategy to prevent getting caught up in these doldrums. Stay on schedule by getting up early, keeping a morning routine, and starting work on time. While it's acceptable to make little tweaks here and there as necessary, maintaining a regular schedule will keep you from feeling continually rushed.

3. Take breaks frequently during the day.

It might seem unnecessary to take a break while you're working from home while your pet is curled up on your lap and you're wearing cozy pajamas. You might even eat while completing tasks or participating in meetings. On the other hand, it's unhealthy to spend the entire day focusing on a screen for long periods. Even remote workers need to take breaks. It will not only break up your day but has been shown to increase productivity.

Get away from your displays and go for a stroll outside, stop by a nearby coffee shop, or have a quick snack while you're offline for a while. According to research, it's optimal for your health to take breaks for 12 percent of each workday. Therefore, if you work eight hours every day, you should take a break for about 58 minutes.

On your breaks, it's crucial to move around. It's crucial to move when you can to be healthy because you aren't moving around as much for meetings or during the day.

4. **Obtain the appropriate tools for the job.**

If you spend the entire day checking many screens while working on a laptop, it may not be the best setup. Additionally, it's not the most ergonomic answer. Inquire about purchasing more computer displays, wireless keyboards and mouse, speakers, printers, and any other office supplies you might require if you work for a company.

Purchasing the equipment that increases your productivity will enhance your workdays if you are a freelancer. A comfortable chair or a workstation that easily changes from a sitting to a standing position can both enhance your ability to work remotely.

5. **Keep in touch and be social.**

When you work for a firm remotely, it might be challenging to interact with coworkers because you are not physically present. The amount of contact isn't always the same, even when you have conference calls.

Maintain interest in your work by interacting with coworkers throughout the day. Engage in video calls, send occasional chats, and assist when you see that another colleague is struggling. To become more involved at work, speak with your manager and be sure to inquire about any new possibilities or optional team meetings. Get social as well. To get to know your coworkers better outside of business hours, host or participate in virtual hangouts or happy hours.

This may be a little more challenging if you freelance because you'll frequently be working with clients rather than coworkers. Any clients who are expecting you to submit work should receive clear communication throughout the day. If there is ever any confusion, make sure to clarify things. Through social media, you can connect with other local freelancers in your area who share your interests so that you have a group to share ideas with and ask for guidance from.

REMOTE JOB OPPORTUNITIES

Copywriter - There are many different types of copywriters who work remotely, from independent freelancers and part-time writers to full-time marketing copywriters. Writing is a job that lends itself naturally to working from home because it can be done online. This position pays an average salary of $50,570.

Recruiter - A recruiter aids job seekers in locating the greatest openings available. In addition to generating job descriptions, evaluating applicants, and networking, recruiters may work for an organization or a particular business. This job pays an average of about $49,554.

Virtual Assistant - A virtual assistant is a person who supports a business owner, entrepreneur, or executive in managing their daily activities. Depending on the requirements of their business, their daily duties could vary, but a typical day might involve setting up meetings, organizing travel, taking notes during meetings, and liaising with other parties. This position typically pays $39,617 annually.

Marketing Manager - Since more and more marketing firms allow employees to work remotely, this profession is perfect for anyone who wants to try out remote employment. These managers may be in charge of a group of creatives or oversee the execution of particular campaigns and business plans for customers. Approximately $64,500 is the going rate for this position.

Curriculum Designers - Developing a curriculum for teachers is a full-time job in and of itself. For schools and other educational institutions, curriculum designers organize, develop, and create curricula. They frequently work remotely. The typical salary for this occupation is about $61,389 per year.

Customer Support Specialist - It's simple to locate a remote job that's perfect for you if you have experience in providing excellent customer support. Home-based customer service representatives may take phone calls from clients, respond to web chats, or provide video help. Additionally, they could use social media or email to communicate. Around $41,382 is what this position typically pays in salary.

Translator - If you speak another language well, you may work from home as a translator. Written materials will be translated from one language to another by translators. They might also convert audio files into written text while simultaneously translating. Around $49,974 is the typical salary for this occupation.

Social Media Manager - Managers that specialize in social media initiatives on websites like Facebook, LinkedIn, and Instagram are known as social media managers. They assist in growing social media presence and website traffic for businesses, creating new initiatives, and monitoring participation. Managers of social media frequently operate from home or in an office. Around $49,881 is the typical salary for this occupation.

Designer - Designers, particularly web designers, frequently have the flexibility to work from any location. The majority of businesses that hire designers permit them to work remotely, whether they are creating designs for marketing materials, websites, or apps. Around $49,649 is the typical salary for this job.

Developers - Developers frequently choose quiet workspaces so they can focus on writing sophisticated code and resolving challenging business problems. Particularly front-end web engineers frequently have the option to work remotely, whether for an employer or on their own. This position pays an average salary of about $71,145.

These are just a few of the many jobs that frequently allow for remote work. Additionally, there are plenty of remote employment opportunities in the accounting, medical, and educational sectors.

CHAPTER FOUR

BIG LIST OF POSITIONS

TYPES OF HOME-BASED JOBS

Both online and offline, there are many various kinds of work-from-home employment. To determine which professions match your interests and skills, you must conduct research. You can work from home as a freelancer, independent contractor, or employee, depending on the type of employment you select. The most sought-after work-from-home positions are in the following categories:

• Writing articles for blogs and websites.

• Editing.

• Proofreading.

• Copywriting.

• Translating.

- Transcription.

- Interpreting.

- Customer service.

- Call centers.

- Virtual assistants.

- Data entry.

- Internet marketers.

- Online chat and email.

- Search engine evaluators.

- Web designers.

- Graphic designers.

- Search engine optimizers.

- Social media consultants.

- Online tutoring.

- Accounting and bookkeeping.

IDEAS FOR HOME-BASED BUSINESSES

There are many excellent options for a home-based business if you want to be your boss. Check out these opportunities, which are listed below:

- Blogging

- Freelance Writing

- Website or blog creation

- eBook creation

- eBay product sales

- Information or digital product sales

- Online sales of tangible goods

- Affiliate marketing business

- Translation

- Web design business

- Virtual assistant business

- Medical billing

- Freelance photography business

BEST SITES FOR FINDING WORK FROM HOME JOB

You can discover these kinds of in-demand jobs by using websites that let you work from home. Due to the high demand for remote employment, be wary of websites that advertise fake job postings and other types of fraud.

These websites are the ideal place to begin if you're wondering how to find a job that allows you to work from home because each one specifically lists positions that allow for remote work as a primary requirement.

Indeed.com

Indeed, a popular website for traditional job searching also has a section dedicated to remote employment opportunities. More than 135,000 remote job openings are currently available on the website, which allows you to search by job type, salary range, location, employer, and level of experience. Users can upload their resumes to Indeed so that employers can locate them.

ZipRecruiter

Despite being a broader employment market that also posts chances for regular work, ZipRecruiter has a section dedicated to remote jobs. More than 295,000 remote jobs were available in its database as of late November.

The site lists many popular remote job categories, including contract, part-time, and administrative work. Teacher, graphic designer, and bookkeeper are some of the most sought-after remote job descriptions on the website.

Working Nomads

By providing a global remote employment board, Working Nomads sets itself apart from competing websites. It offers not only remote opportunities but also partially remote ones where you might need to spend some time on-site for training or team-building objectives. It targets job searchers who need "only a computer, Wi-Fi, and a cloud" to complete their work.

FlexJobs

One of the first websites developed to assist professionals in finding remote and flexible jobs is FlexJobs. Sara Sutton, the founder of the website, claims that the abundance of fake job sites in this market deterred her from starting FlexJobs. She had been looking for remote work with a flexible schedule while pregnant.

Opportunities are available from entry-level to executive levels, including part-time and full-time. The company offers a money-back guarantee and client support to its customers. For a one-week trial, pricing begins at $6.95.

Remote.co

A FlexJobs partner and website for "all things remote work," Remote.co, was established by Sutton as well. There are areas for both job seekers and employers to post remote job openings.

Additionally, there is a blog about remote work on the website, and 142 virtual teams and remote businesses respond to frequently asked questions about working from home.

CHAPTER FIVE

TYPES OF WORK YOU CAN DO FROM HOME

Many opportunities have opened up for those who work from home through the internet. The internet can help you earn extra money, purchase a computer, learn skills, or work on your own time. You need to be aware of all the available options to create a plan that suits your needs and goals. There are many options for people to use their work-from-home experience.

Get paid to post on social media

Posting updates, producing videos, and sharing content can be relatively easy ways to create passive income.

Make an online course

This is another way to make some extra money at home. There are many opportunities, whether you're teaching others about computer programming or cooking.

You can find freelance work

This is a popular option for artists and writers looking to make extra money. You can find this type of work on various websites, but make sure you only use trusted sites.

Write reviews and take pictures

Many places will pay you for what you love, whether you're a photographer, writer, or entrepreneur. Register for Opinion Outpost and eLotto.

Get paid to flex on the internet

Flexibility on the internet can earn you a commission: **FlexOffer** and **Poshmark** allow you to sell your products online without going through traditional retail stores. Although it's not easy, selling online can be a great way to make money at home.

You can also take surveys to make money

This is another way to make money at home. **Survey Junkie**, **Swagbucks**, and other sites are well-known for offering reliable survey opportunities. Before you begin taking part, make sure to review the sites thoroughly.

Browse the internet

Many tasks will pay you to browse, and some of them can even be very fun. You can earn money by performing simple tasks on your computer through Onetangl and InstaGC.

Start a blog

If you are passionate about writing or something, a popular blog could be a great way to make money online. Although it can be difficult to get started due to the competition online, becoming a blogger is possible.

Get paid to test

UserTesting offers a way to get paid for your feedback. Although it's not the most exciting, it can be very effective.

Write an ebook

An eBook is a hard task but can also be extremely profitable. This type of venture can be lucrative if you are willing to put in the effort and time.

Earn money to direct video

Videogames are very popular at the moment. If you're looking to make a name for yourself by being an expert in this field, creating game walkthroughs can be a great way to do so. You can find places like YTGameWalk. Byte Me. and 99Monsters.

Making money on eBay

Selling your unwanted items on eBay can be a great way to make money from home. Although it's not something that you can do every day, it could be a way to help you reach your ultimate goals.

Sell apps and develop them

The internet is becoming more competitive. If you're looking to make a living from your home by selling apps, many companies will pay cash for every download. App-making sites like Fiverr and Upwork will pay you to create apps. You can also create one and see how it works if you have an idea.

Write articles

It would be a good idea to make this hobby a business. However, with so much competition online, it can prove difficult. Many websites will pay you to create articles on niche subjects or expert advice from larger companies.

Get paid to interact

Websites like eLotto & Opinion Outpost. These sites offer cash rewards for correctly answering simple questions. This could be a great way to make some extra cash.

You can become an internet marketer

This is a great way to make a living and hit the jackpot. Many sites will pay you to market their products online. Many of these sites are legit, but you should make sure to review them and ensure that you feel safe using them.

Earn money for giving your opinion on products

Sites such as Opinion Outpost, eLotto, and Swagbucks all offer the opportunity to make money from providing feedback. This can be a great way to make extra money while gaining experience in the industry.

Write product reviews

Websites such as CJ, Get Paid Reviews & eLotto pay you to write detailed product reviews. Although it's not difficult to work, it can take some time. Also, these sites are part of affiliate programs that pay a percentage of each sale.

You can sell videos

Fiverr, Upwork and others will pay you to make simple videos. This could be a great opportunity to make money if you are skilled in video production. Make sure that you only accept jobs worth what you claim they will pay.

Logo design

Although it might seem difficult to start, it can be a great way to make extra money. Many websites will pay you to design a logo.

Create business cards

Sites like Upwork, Fiverr, and 99 Designs all allow you to create business cards for a decent fee. If you need a new one, you can grab yourself some extra cash by creating your own.

Snap pictures

It's worth starting as a freelance photographer if you are skilled with a camera. Shutterstock.com pays you for each image you upload, and if you have a lot of followers, this could be a great way to make some extra cash.

Redirect traffic

This can make you a lot of money at home. Websites that have problems with their internet are usually being hacked. If you have the skills to make this happen, you can be paid to redirect their website, so it is secure again.

Host domains

This is a great way to make money at home if you have the time. Dotster.com will grant you a domain name for the life of your choice if you can do it correctly. Perfect for making money online.

Modify PDF files

This is a great way to make extra cash. You can modify PDF documents on 99 Designs, Upwork, and Fiverr sites. This could be a great way to make money at home if you have previous experience.

You can get paid to write

Many companies on the internet sound too good to be true. Many websites offer money for writing quality articles. Versatile is one the most popular sites, with a wide range of articles and ads.

Earn money for commenting

Swagbucks has its own "bounty program" where you can answer questions and give feedback about products to earn free money. They pay in real cash and even pay to refer friends to other network members.

Make an infographic

This is a great way to make money at home if you are good at creating infographics. You can earn extra money by creating infographics on 99 Designs, Visual.ly, and Airtable.

You can test websites

Many companies will pay you to test websites and apps before they go live. Swagbucks and 99 Designs offer points for testing websites. Upwork, 99 Designs, and 99 Designs pay for app testing.

Code

This could be a great way to make extra income from home if you enjoy coding. CodeAcademy and Codeable will let you earn money using your programming skills.

Make ads

You can create ads on sites like Fiverr or Upwork. Just make sure the site is legitimate before you start.

Translate

While this is a difficult way to make money online, it can also be lucrative if you have the time.

Make art

99 Designs pays you to create images. This could be a great way to make money at home if you're skilled

.

Conclusion

More sites are being created every day to offer people like you the opportunity to work remotely. These job opportunities are available through name-brand sites. You can also search for work-at-home companies to explore other career options.

If you enjoyed this book, I will really appreciate a five star rating.

Made in the USA
Las Vegas, NV
18 September 2022

55554871R00046